Natural Disasters

Avalanches

by Julie Murray

3

Dash!
LEVELED READERS

An Imprint of Abdo Zoom • abdobooks.com

Dash!
LEVELED READERS

Level 1 – Beginning
Short and simple sentences with familiar words or patterns for children who are beginning to understand how letters and sounds go together.

Level 2 – Emerging
Longer words and sentences with more complex language patterns for readers who are practicing common words and letter sounds.

Level 3 – Transitional
More developed language and vocabulary for readers who are becoming more independent.

THIS BOOK CONTAINS RECYCLED MATERIALS

abdobooks.com

Published by Abdo Zoom, a division of ABDO, PO Box 398166, Minneapolis, Minnesota 55439.

Printed in the United States of America, North Mankato, Minnesota.
052024
092024

Photo Credits: Getty Images, Shutterstock
Production Contributors: Kenny Abdo, Jennie Forsberg, Grace Hansen, John Hansen
Design Contributors: Candice Keimig, Neil Klinepier

Library of Congress Control Number: 2023948494

Publisher's Cataloging in Publication Data

Names: Murray, Julie, author.
Title: Avalanches / by Julie Murray
Description: Minneapolis, Minnesota : Abdo Zoom, 2025 | Series: Natural disasters | Includes online resources and index.
Identifiers: ISBN 9781098285494 (lib. bdg.) | ISBN 9781098286194 (ebook) | ISBN 9781098286545 (Read-to-me eBook)
Subjects: LCSH: Natural disasters--Juvenile literature. | Avalanches--Juvenile literature. | Winter storms--Juvenile literature. | Snow--Juvenile literature.
Classification: DDC 904.5--dc23

Table of Contents

Avalanches

An avalanche is the sudden rush of a large amount of snow down a slope. It happens when a layer of snow collapses and breaks away. The snow gains speed and strength as it moves down the slope.

Avalanches are powerful events that can be deadly. They often sweep up trees, rocks, and anything else in their paths. They can bury homes and buildings too.

Causes

Avalanches take place on steep slopes. Slopes can be on hills or mountains. Most avalanches happen after a major snow event.

Changes in temperature can weaken snow layers. This makes the layers more likely to separate. Weather, an earthquake, or human movement can act as the **trigger** for an avalanche.

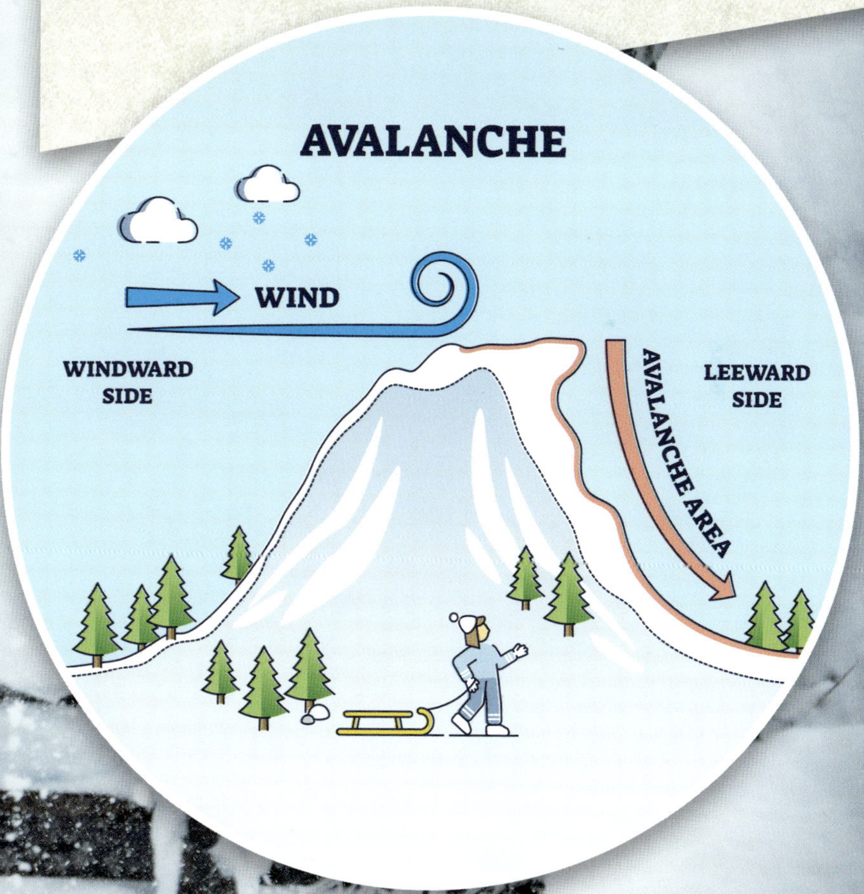

An avalanche has three main parts. The starting zone is where the avalanche begins. The avalanche track is the path it travels downhill.

The runout zone is where the avalanche ends. Snow and **debris** pile up here.

Types of Avalanches

There are three types of avalanches. A powder avalanche is made of loose, powdery snow. It usually causes little damage. A wet avalanche is slow moving. The snow is heavy and has great force as it moves.

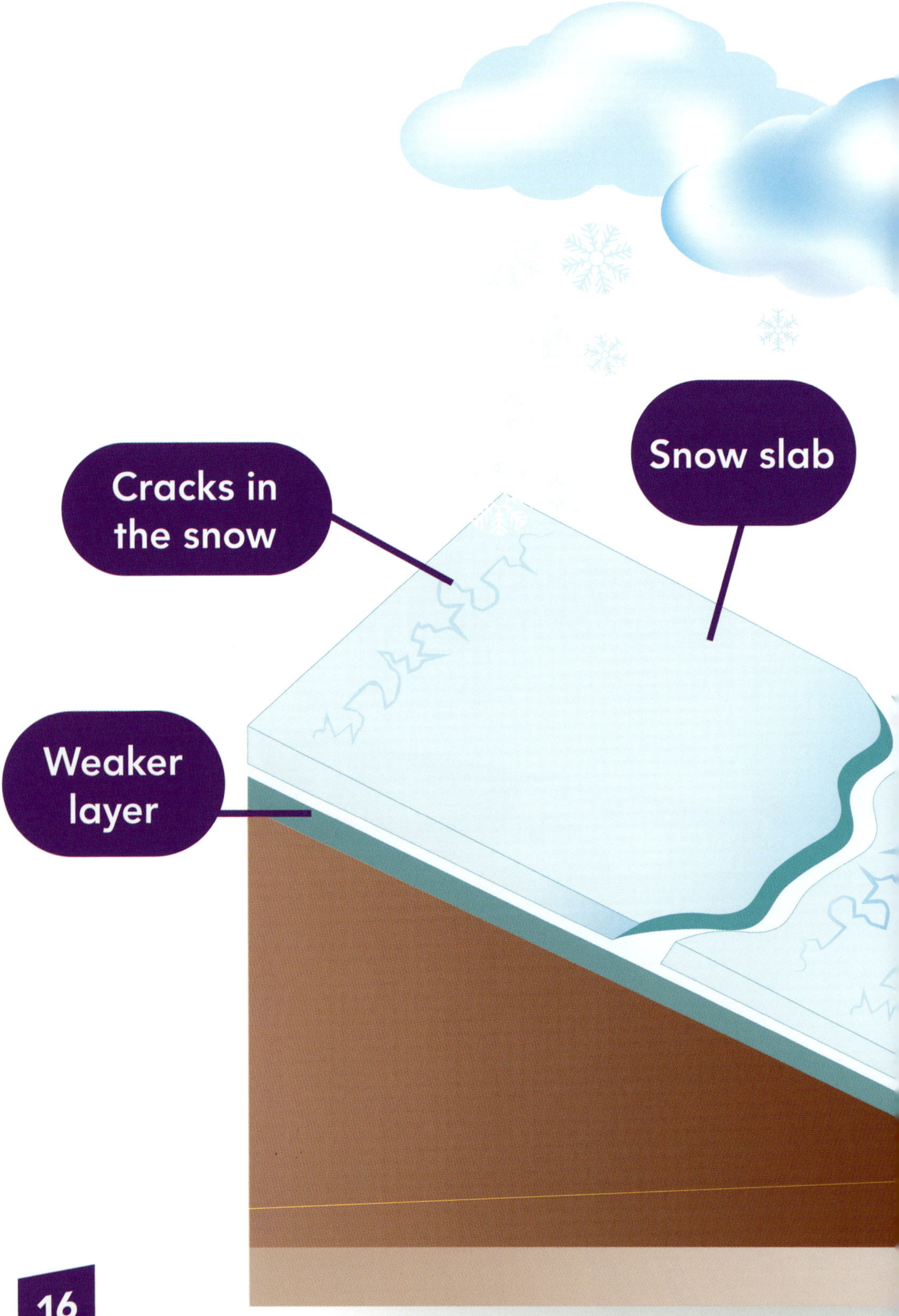
Snow slab
Cracks in the snow
Weaker layer

A slab avalanche is the most dangerous. This happens when a large slab of snow breaks free. It can travel up to 200 miles per hour (322 kph)!

Ski patrol teams closely **monitor** conditions. They issue warnings near unsafe areas. They also perform controlled avalanches. They carefully **trigger** small avalanches to prevent a larger one.

CLOSED
AVALANCHE
DANGER
CLOSED
Trespassers will be
Prosecuted

Ski patrol teams search for people caught in an avalanche. Search dogs also help. The teams use **probes** and shovels. They can find people buried under the snow. They save many lives each year!

More Facts

- More than 150 people lose their lives in avalanches every year.
- Avalanches can carry up to 300,000 cubic yards (230,000 cubic meters) of snow. This is equal to 20 football fields covered in 10 feet (3.05 m) of snow!
- People can wear a rescue beacon in avalanche-prone areas. This device sends out a signal so a person can be located faster if caught in an avalanche.

Glossary

debris – scattered pieces left after something has been destroyed.

monitor – to observe in order to check on.

probe – an instrument or tool used to explore the shape, condition, or depth of something that cannot be seen directly.

trigger – to cause, begin, or set off.

Index

Online Resources

Booklinks
NONFICTION NETWORK
FREE! ONLINE NONFICTION RESOURCES

To learn more about Avalanches, please visit **abdobooklinks.com** or scan this QR code. These links are routinely monitored and updated to provide the most current information available.